CIRC

CIRCLE TIME

SAM RAWLINGS

Lazy Gramophone Press

Copyright © Sam Rawlings 2005

Designed and illustrated by Dan Prescott

The moral right of the author has been asserted

A CIP catalogue record of this book is
available from the British Library

First published in 2006 by Lazy Gramophone Press,
part of the ineffable Lazy Gramophone collective

Fourth edition 2010

ISBN: 9771473968012

www.lazygramophone.com

For Foetus

'Four or five men dance in a circle
Above them
The moon is about to drop'

Buson Yosa
1716-1783

CONTENTS

Autumn

The Mornings Keep Falling

Mornings trapped inside raindrops
Keep falling on my head

October

I can feel the murmurs of change
almost touch them:
a single nerve.
Visceral as time
their light brushes of space against my skin,
an idiot's wind
afloat upon the hems of destiny.
As cradled arms
the depths of your eyes hide me, stow me away.

Safely enclosed in romance
the moments wait.

Hymn

Clouds might hold hands
but that doesn't mean they should be believed or trusted.
Branches stir, emerge from their falling leaves
it's that time of year again,
they'll never learn.
Stones couldn't careless.
Impartial the sea sulks
still undecided
while the sky retires to its room,
earlier and earlier after each round
before rolling into another;
another today as is our habit
the traffic made of somewhere else.
Hours change with their spelling,
still kicking around

clockwise from kiss to kiss.

Dustbin Lids

Hope-rings frame our dirty dustbin lids
as we sit and smoke on the scarred tarmac.
Bored it falls through the throats of our trucks,
sore from so many learnt lessons but
still we pour our drawings all over the side walk.
The asphalt rumbles
mumbles sarcastically through hollow ears,
as we carve our tears within the cold and cracked carpets
been laid to free us?
Please us? Lead us astray?
At least they take us away from here for a while.
For miles the rhythmic street lamps fill our eyes
with time at last, as curbs dive and rise
slip by beneath our meaningless lives;
so light tonight below the black 'n' heavy sky.

Rebel

A yellow puddle
adrift the persistence,
lock of hair, of refuge
accorded the blinking sky.
                    My light of air.

Town of teeth and darkness, another haunted morning,
echoes of a thousand feet, black eyes and perfect manes,
the sound of our pause, the sound of change.
My weight a damn of silence against the roar of space.
She stands
with balanced lips, our seesaw aches.

My ashen canvas curled beneath her
as if a feather fallen, line of chalk,
a single flame drawn from the pale of dawn

she hesitates.

Gathered Up

Gathered up
the sun is gone from here.
Has been seduced by the winter moods
by the whispering blue
merging slowly with impending black.
Addicted to the canvas of peace fallen
expression squirms,
stands abandoned and calling.
Repression quickly hoarding us all into our homes.

Betrayal

Mindful of the silence we tip toe across the ice,
warm within our palms our secret,
still safe and still small its limbs curled with guilt.
Shy of the world we creep to keep its peace.

Wind delivers itself upon each ear.
In turn it whispers offers of a truce, a fare
exchange for diverting our trembling smell,
our lie through tonight's tunnel of dark eyes.

Smiles flicker upon our lips
as silhouettes reassure our hearts
heave each others blood.
Deep inside stubborn tears hold time, with patience wait
reluctantly for tomorrow to arrive.

Already

Autumn's secrets
have begun to nestle in your hair,
your lids fall, lips softened by the sullen sky.
I won't need the frost upon my window
this year as a reason to,
this year already
I've fallen in love with you.

Quiet

Take a little time.
Open your eyes and gather your breath.
The dark has passed morning come once again
to play on the frosty ground of tonight's
apprehensive death.
Winter blues hang white from the leaves of trees;
and it may be late
but it feels so early,
under the infant naivety of the perfect roundness of the moon
within the undeveloped purity of a playful breeze.
This beauty so simple, noticed too infrequently
its silence over too soon.

Welcome Home

I'm leaving before it's too late
but my eyes will grace you again

happiness, relax upon your beautiful shoulders
bury into the deep beneath your chin.

I will be the whispering
within your ears.

The humming moon
soft as sleep in a tonight's sky.

The inherent blandness of repetition
From womb to womb the passing power of decision
Her words turned from the universe light as flame
The pages burn our patience breathes
These incubus
An heirloom

Empathy
A cadence peeked
Our vision born as eyes from dreams
Death of an echo sing the rings of vibration
Upon an empty canvas upon an empty stage
A singular colour of differing shade

The inherent blandness of repetition
From womb to womb the passing power of decision
Her words turned from the universe light as flame
The pages burn our patience breathes
These incubus
An heirloom

Empathy
A cadence peeked
Our vision born as eyes from dreams
Death of an echo sing the rings of vibration
Upon an empty canvas upon an empty stage
A singular colour of differing shade

Until Morning

As the stars die
I don't know whether to laugh or cry.
It all seems so sad but it happens like clockwork
and so I continue to sit,
upon this porch easing my mind with mugs of coffee
and chocolate.

Winter

This Place

This place,
where it all was
and will never be haunts me,
deepens my footsteps almost proudly.

The Weight

The wrinkles are beginning to show
upon our words,
as they're turned over
and over again within our mouths
before each of our faces.

Sentiment clings to our seconds
becomes the crumbs sleeping in our laps,
lost beneath the cracks of floorboards.

We stare.
Out from inside each other.
Await the beginning of yet another dream
to tow us away. Please.
For we can see flowers

behind each flinch of our eyes; beginning to realise
that they'll no longer grow only outside that window
as the nights continue to close around our wrists.

Memories of all we'll miss slip from our lips
parents fingers entwine,
tears toward the ground.
Towards our black
finally.

Someday

New born
scattered puffs of air
dance like angels again this morning,
as they slip from between our warm lips
and out into the icy sky still sleepy,
still hanging weakly onto last night.

With trust once more our dreams play
with memories, as the moon slowly departs,
her tears and her kisses paint the dawn;
filled with regret at the yawning sun so close

yet always so far away.
To smiles someday to a beginning
maybe our old eyes will rise,
peaceful and free from these sad
drunken waterfalls
hatching.

Robbery

The door of the vault is flapping in the wind
yards from the house,
dumped in the long grass at the foot of that mound
where as a child I'd sat.

Heavy wood, twisted and pulled from its hinges
lay injured. Torn from the wall.
Old black at last allowed to crawl free
with squinting eyes once again witness the ocean;
forgotten already that smell of rotting seaweed
still safe within his pocket.

The window panes are cracked
glass cold now, fallen effeminately from its hold.
Though each shared still breathes:
their rise and falls so pretty
within the dark.

I hear stones click
and then echo.
Bricks are crumbling
the house slowly dripping into the mist.
Wide and flat mother's tracks limp into the distance,
giant hands finally sagging
tired from her squat frame.

Spread too thin
the slate aches
chimney gasps for air.
With limbs bruised and so empty
tears rip from the sky
add yet more salt to the sea,
down upon the fields surrounding me.
A naked sack of bone
layers of home left scattered behind my body.

Tidal

…. for it's you
    I belong to.

        Our goodbyes
        are like straight lines
        they deceive our eyes
        neither exist,
        all bow eventually into curves
        and turn with the world.
        Even the longest
        are only parts of even larger circles.

        And so wait with me
        and meet me there,
        somewhere without sun or moon
        for it's you

    I belong to.
Our goodbyes …

When I

Can feel the ache within waiting,
the impatience jolting my shoulders
rattling my ribs and thumping my diligent heart.

Starting to realise that even if I do,
it's not going to stop.
My wick will be revealed
my skin peeled and my flesh stripped,
left clinging to the knobbles upon each humble ankle.
Until only the jangle of my hanging fingertips,
the trail of my limp tongue, discarded feet,
will be left to echo beneath
the growing weight of so many hours.

There will be no lingering piles of smiles
hiding behind perfect teeth.
No pools of unused tears
seeping through my ears when I die.

Inland

Crumbles like the dry leaves beneath my feet
the scenery around here.
Trampled and bitter to taste
to touch there's too much concrete.
So many corners:
too many maybes within each day.

Peeling back the claustrophobic fields
I wish I could steal a glimpse of my stolen blue canvas,
skim those piles of pebbles gathering
behind my eyes.

They're lonely and falling,
those grains of sand
still stuck between my toes
clinging to my clothes,

for how long can one winter last.

Sometimes Sadly

Today was never meant to,
a never's end;
a doorway,
an apparition,
just for pretend;
and so let the yesterdays commence
for only tomorrows lament
without asking.

The Missing

Our faces sing discreetly
scattered beneath the moonlight,
behind their splintered window panes.

Faint shadows stalk the sidewalks,
voices echo.
The sounds of boots only a whisper
their nets fallen forever now, hunt the ocean floor,
while strong hips and delicate fingertips
slip secretly still through overgrown orchards.

Absinthe skies
sensibly water the sunflowers
transparent in our absence.

Shy

The solemn oaths of secrecy
sewn into the cuts across my arms
laugh so loud sometimes
that I can feel my T-shirt growing shy
under everyone's enquiring eyes.

Of Storms

Clouds scatter temporary memories,
as if time isn't short enough
draw puddles from the ground.
Our reflections skip between each open window;
each no more than an old bottle top, a teardrop
upon a row.

Slowly

Beneath her crispy hair
the frost slips slowly from her lips
as the icicles begin to melt
drip from her frozen eyes,
the snow only
as high as her knees now
all alone
within her pure white
desert where no footsteps
have ever before been allowed to fall.

So careful each incision he makes
each drag of air he takes
placating her moon as he moves
shy eyes to the ground.
To bow?
Or to rise and kiss her?

Spring

Sunshine

His cloud will want to grow
Her blue frost bloom
Every kiss
A cold vacation from the sound of dreaming

Thought I Saw Your Face

While watching the day fade
I thought I saw your face grace the setting sun.
So then within the colliding colours of its mellow glow
I planted a seed of hope,
made a wish that you'd grow from the falling morning
next time it sulks through my window.
As beautifully as only a fairy tale could sow
I dreamt a while,
about how you'd smile
and then kiss me;
before wishing all of my missing you away.

I Love U

Trying to work
on a sunny day and you're so far away,
and I love you
I love you I love you
I love you I love you
'I love U's
are floating around in my head,
and it's only for your beautiful smile
that they are being written to be read.

Spring

Pregnant tonight's belly bulges
with all who still remain.
Bound in promises the hours slowly undress,
dance beneath the dripping shadows
while words paint their slender silhouettes.
Compliments hang tenderly from ear lobes
decorate shy cheeks soft from knowing.
Innocent lips bewitch as they flinch from listening
sink seductively beneath politely blinking eyes.
Pristine white teeth slice through premature tongues but
tomorrow morning has already begun to rise
the goodnight sunlight settle;
upon travelled skin still smouldering
upon a tranquil canvas of deep blue sleep
and dreams breaking over new born limbs.

Last Night

Plundered the deep
black sky last night;
am hiding the moon behind my eyes.

Love

Was surprised by the sunrise surfacing
from behind your gentle brown eyes.
The warmth suddenly resting upon my lies
I didn't realise,
would be so beautiful.

Laudanum

Broken fences and bumblebees
a fumbling breeze,
green grass giggles
and white lilies frequent the early open blue
born above our insomnia.
Palm in palm our fingertips kiss,
our footsteps clap,
our eyes and lips and teeth splash
all over these moments.
Amongst the trees and the listening peace so pleasant,
polite this morning guides our fumbling,
stumbling, lingering lives
towards something a little more legitimate.

Jealousy

When she walks slow
And I walk fast,
She looks at me
As I do at her,
With jealousy
At the speed of which we've decided to pass our time.

You Are

You are as precious,
as beautiful,
as a single raindrop
within the endless heat of so many sunny days.
You are my reason to believe in when,
are why mornings keep falling
so hopefully,
over and over
again.

Painters

I'm the only one could ever paint you
sculpt your pieces into the beauty they deserve,
pick your broken petals and decorate the rain in daisy chains
wrap you up in sky.
Lay your body within a bed of stars
the night a blank canvas for your hearts playful art,
until; morning impatient and pouring kisses
curious on the other side of your eyelids can't resist
and lifts, gentle yawning replacing the drawing
as sunshine nuzzles in.
Your placid smiles a warning
of another day
as we slowly wake.

X

She wears secrets in her hair
it's that time of year,
when children splash in the puddles of the blue of her eyes.

If she ever speaks she shines
words like stars stolen from the night;
and so it feels as alright as when the sun's in the sky
like the distant hum of a rainy day
the silence after speaking when everything's been said and made.

Like the perfect yellow of a yellow morning
and the endlessness of summertime
She is
and it's as alright as when.

Portrait

With rusted charm
These poems for the asking,
A premise for beautiful memories.
That collage of shadow,
Where mysteries smoulder
Smoke with age.
Vines of chalk
And clouds fall away.

Summer

Sun Shy

Please believe me.
It's you only that I love;
beneath the souls of my naked feet
now stretched towards the sky
as we lye upon our backs.

Eyes relaxed
thoughts full and proud
staple my head to the ground,
bleached by the taste of you.

White still from winter
blushing still
as I continue to miss her

so much.

Sticky & Sweet

Urgency slows
as love melts all sticky and sweet
like chocolate on days like these;
beneath the chalky lines
been scratched across today's pure blue sky;
beneath the egg yolk dripping
dropping blonde locks of tongue,
almost ticklish as they lick us.

Thirsty

Can almost see today's heat.
Dirt crumbles from my grey tongue,
from my dry mouth and spills out
from between my chapped lips
before dropping to the dusty brown ground
been laid for miles all-around me;
and you again
this morning.

Decadence

The endless pounding of skin upon road,
dry, burnt and dusty is beginning to take its toll on me.
Cheeks smile no longer.
Hungry, I love her hot summer,
I wonder with obstinance
and salty fingernails.
I sing steadily,
without air for breath,
I forget; my glue at last grown soft in the heat.
Today has begun to peel from me,
its corners flapping in the breeze.
Bored of those same pale tones of faded surface
my hours grow fervent for fresher, more exotic meat.
A sigh so thick her eyes will surely now
sit cold and empty;
as two ethereal memories,
dry, burnt and dusty, beautiful her smile,
before swallowing me.

Hung

Within the lamp light
Huddled around her and me
And this lonely table,
Humble within tonight's kitchen
Of wood and of no sleep,
Our eyes swell to double their usual size
And words crumble before
They can even begin to stumble from our lips.
The pits of our stomachs have grown sour
From so many hours
But still we continue to feed.
Could picture this scene
Displayed on a wall.
After all we've both paid enough for it;
For the baisse noir lighting
For the violence silent so beautiful between us,
For the slits across our wrists
Sown simply now by its title.
If only this frame wasn't so fragile,
Then maybe one day we
Could have hung it.

This Summer

Blue Skies hang in-between my nights
As shapeless lakes of space in time they lie
Lightly suspended but heavy with wait
Beautiful and wasted without you

The Warmth of Rain

Crouched below
those lowered tones
of voice, broad shoulders and pieces of mind
clouds to my sky. I smile.
For the holes in my bones
holes in my pockets,
the absence of home,
of love, misty lungs
that could never be enough
mere incense, my decadence.
My lantern, those flickers of romance,
the yellow in my blood.

Ignored

The forgotten shoals
of broken shards of stars sing so quietly,
that it is only in times like these
their melody can be heard
whispering defiantly;
their violent lullabies shaping the shadows
breaking so softly over this evenings shore.
No longer completely ignored
at least.

Lost

These are crazy days
these days of no sleep,
time as sparse as the sunshine
my mind growing with all I see.
So full am I that both eyes and ears leak.
Buried within my own avalanche
I fear the inability to think.
Unsure, but reassured by a lack of reason,
my doubts I worry are being abducted by the tide
their breath stolen, eyes silenced.
The horizon sings
I'm falling in.

By Hope

Shouldn't we speak a little more softly
afloat the breeze,
in case words like memories conspire to break this,
reclaim our hearts.
Locks of chaos fall, dance upon her neck,
arc of chin and that quick inhalation of breath;
a labyrinth of limbs.

Shouldn't we pay a little more attention
cling a little tighter to this skimming stone's mast,
for thoughts perchance to kiss, so often surpassed
amid the mesh of rings flowering so fast.
An angel's wings, the raising of her arms
the curl of her lips, soil slipped from view. I
love you. Two roots torn from the ground.
Living proof, our rebellion.

Motionless for now, her petals float before me
though still she meets my eyes;
a single wish upon an ocean so vast,
so defenceless yet still our whispers laugh.
Nothing but the rhythm of the waves.

Cast adrift, so slowly we begin again
our paddle toward the shore.

Escape

The sun clings this afternoon
to my back
nestles in-between the notches of my spine,
so cold,
and sharp the air feels already
though my eyelids continue to swim.
Limbs seduced by those tribal whisperings
that pass as clouds
those same shy white flags of morning.

Blood stains my naked feet
street numb and bone
upon the land.
I continue to listen

but still my mouth cannot fathom
the disappearance of so many things all at once,
fingernails placate the soil into growing freckles upon my skin.

Chambers deflated and the mosquitoes satisfied
my pump whistles
air in spite of your weight: 'Pilgrime'
return to the shade.
Blue as water my lung's song
silent as the open sky.
Afraid only of tonight and the close of my own two eyes
in case I find that even on the inside

It has always been this obvious.

Craving

Childish escape plays
unsafe and vulnerable upon hopeful days made only of waiting,
of humbling hours trailing off tiredly
towards confiding silently
  once again.

For this room I have,
its walls shaped so perfectly,
this room is a star.
It is my future, it is my past.
This room I have is my home, soft and sincere,
it is all that belongs to me.
It is where I dream you will one day hold me,
whisper sweetly into my ear.
This room I have is the moment you say you love me,
is the second those words
I finally hear

and so cradle me sleep,
and dreams
of white like lily things
lined with lullabies

and time
I'm tired
of being. Susceptible
to the appeal of the softness lying behind your eyes,
my moon. I can hear the drum of your slender fingers,
a choir so perfectly in time to lullabies and rhyme rising;
an arsenal of flowers
yet still I am powerless before you.
Could never placate
even the prettier hours.
Such hate,
the romance of our maybes held fast,
a spark caged
an endless dance no chance
of sleep thanks to the still remains of another sunny day.
The cars didn't stop until at least two
every engine interrupting a thought of you;
and it is not really as silent as you would think late at night,
feelings sing, consequences ring and like mirrors
sound reflects everything I do.
It was peaceful though as everyone slept
inside that house,

around my muffled crunch of cereal
and below the imminence of another thunderstorm.

Yet the mornings will bring you,
freshly tumbled, pebble smooth from sleep.
A puddle at my side,
unwrapped by the light you emerge, white as the walls,
with the brown of the floorboards,
alongside the traffic's calls.
The dripping sky as small as the balls of your feet.
This, the occupation of my smile,
her guile less easily captured.
Trapped inside its own trying
our music naive yet bravely, easily persuaded seeks to concede.

Serving her servants now,
those tiny stitches across my ankles;
they bleed when I attempt to reach her.
Stomach of old,
the cavities within my heart are
dark and hollow.
Your lips like lithium
distil this,
and I know not to appease your taste

with passion
but my achilles are nearly cold.
Blue toes motionless as we stretch to touch
fingertip to fingertip
count each others drips
and fall.

A sour and a bitter sickness
seeps from today's scowl
been ripped open,
been torn open by groping fingers
all stubbornly playing upon our delicious
but vulnerable wishes.
The narrow clouds, sulky red sun,
lacerated sky whose fresh wounds
had only just begun
to heal, now howls;
as once again our eyelids fall
and our minds shy away from this world.
Only the T.V glows
sows so much so carelessly
that I wonder, for how long, can both she and me
continue to remain beneath this blanket been gently thrown over us.
Decorated in dust now our lust

most sensibly concealed
but for the subtlety of her uncoiling;

so sensually
she curls our sounds,
drapes herself gracefully,
gently from above she drips her gaze down,
beautifully violent.
Caressing my naked and bony ears below
been filled with craving
and nothing.

For within the shadows that grow from the depths of her eyes
I see myself in the darkness
can hear only the echoes of my mind.
And within her empty words
that have weighed so heavily upon my life, I can read
but still don't believe in how it's going to be;
don't see any tolerance except my own
don't have any more of an understanding
of how or why it is that I should still feel so alone.
Of why it is that she
has chosen me,
of why it is that my silence has finally settled

lank as the length of her hair,
and even the walls stare can't help but notice
how she wears her crown.
Her peace deep
and as dark as her glare.
A cross-hatch of stitches redden her skin,
a sketch performed with speed
though not without beauty
for the bindings convey tenderness…

…as can a day seem so long.
Need permeates,
a badge of rebellion slung from her bottom lip,
her scars plaster casts of the past
modelled to such cold perfection, this
her answer to him: arching

paralysed with honest over and over
under her
pools of pleasure.

The Freedom Fallen

Music breaks out into the sky
high above the heads,
fills the raindrops with violence
before falling through peoples minds
already so full with regret from so many crimes
but that's life;
and so blood types begin to beat beneath thick layers of skin
burst out and stain grey pavements with the freedom fallen
hoarded for so long now,
glistening red within the sunlight
fuelling the rebellion behind so many squinting eyes, old
sighs examples of why we still try.

This Mourning I

Nothing profound sounds this polite and wiry.
No cures allowed;
They're all around everybody but nobody's telling
Selling instead.
Could live off this stuff
Snort it when lost for words,
When feelings pour towards the exit forgetting
Resigned from upsetting only pretending to talk,
Our intentions are falling;
Lethargic from throats dry and sore
From too much nothing.
Resonant with withdrawn and clouded in cursing
Niggling smashed little grace in
The pretty face,
Hateful and spiteful,
Despite each early morning's new born lie smiling
Heart-breaking out from inside my
I'm, it's a? fine
Line between the hoops hanging
And the belief teasing, threatening to relieve each day.

So full up with insides art colliding with
'Rock 'n' roll' hiding through worth trying for
Got-ten posters of poems fucking
Plastered beneath each fingertip, twitching
And drumming whys while 'I',
Continues to sleep.

Strange Days

It was one of those strange days.
One of those days in which nothing gets done,
and like the hungriest creature decided to stay asleep
and the most naïve child was filled with doubt;
then so did the sun in the sky behind a cloud
decide to lay back down and hide.

The moon also, on the other side of the world
seemed to have a face that cried while all of the stars
as they do sometimes decided to remain out of sight,
deep within their own black sky,
high above what would have been had they eyes, a sad night.

For down below,
    beneath the moon and the stars and the sun in the sky,
still above however
    but only through ignorance because everything dies
the quieter sleeping lives and minds, stood hands on hips a lie.
This misconception though lacked the ability to decide
and so it mealy groaned when questioned with wrong and right,
when proposed with how big to grow and so it endlessly flowed.

With its flow though it made waves
and on these waves provided a stage
and on this stage only the best surfers played;
here on descending peaks they would age would waste todays.

The rest of the world though didn't complain why would they?
For it was apparent that the anarchy of the waves wouldn't stay
and that soon it would come back around to being their day.
So for the meanwhile the sun and the sky
and the lives and the minds
just sighed and didn't mind and enjoyed their break.
Succumbed to the apathy
that there being a virtue in patience had made.

Peace

It is not worth the fight.

All these days of colourful skies and secret nights,
can try as hard as you like, as ruthlessly,
but perfectly early mornings will still rise
drawings of peace continue to haunt the silence behind tear filled
eyes.

It is not worth the fight

when beautiful grows so old
still whispers this defiantly.

War

Our canopy of shade
a fractured whisper with little hope of delay.
Born beneath a sky's shame
leaves tear punctually
branches brake. Amid such weight
those falls of sound discredit the words with which we pray,
set into motion the lungs of those we once so surely maimed.
A balanced fate:
our punctured wind,
life's flinching embrace.

Happy Birthday

Tongues brown then fall
lye dry and with crisp temper accusing
the obstinance of booted feet:
blind and shy of life,
too warm and soft to fight.

Black protrudes slowly
through winter air,
with courteous breath it is agreed
and therefore flames lick the night
mourning still however inside.

A child wipes her eyes
causing travelled tears to collide,
neither cheek solid enough to answer
the echoes of today's news and so our lips muse instead
upon the red raindrops held within each tiny hand.

Rising from these times a blue sunshine
settles heavy this summer upon waking lids.
Without limbs to cast over you I'm sorry

for everything.

Still Looking

They are sad eyes,
those eyes looking at me

filled with emotion
just begging to be set free;

and I've always believed it's in the eyes
and not in the heart
that our feelings are trapped,

some sprinkled with life
some on the verge of collapse.

All so different
yet still so similar to those eyes looking at me

those sad eyes,
perfectly sometimes painfully,
on show for the whole world to see.

Just like those eyes
the sad eyes I can see

those sad eyes still looking at me.

Still Remains

Long have walls stood
and still stones congregate
muttering their vows.
The sound of trying,
a pitter-patter from beneath all of our toes
each planted alone. Apologies
muse silently, eyes raised to the falling snow.
Besieged by the endless clutter
row upon row of orchards grow but so slowly
they climb through the cracks.
Profanity champions the diminishing sky,
each voice a bald halo only peeking
innocently through the white surrender
of a once perfect height.
But the clouds were always going to run hung out like that
upon the flag pole.
For diligence and lies remind
even the mountains sometimes it's true;
let the fingerless accuse.

Mr

Decent now decends to new depths through me.
I had wondered how you slept.
Words burn but still they continue to serve,
march from my mouth,
summon crowds:
I had wondered whether you would ever lay as silently
as we did then,
listen to the quiet?   The questions?
pounds enemies and repentance.
How long did you have to wait
for the echoes to reply?

Deep beneath our exodus, amongst the candles
cast out and into those nights;
Wars end;
that darkness you mourned, had not only been behind those
closed eyes of yours.
at the tips of tongues
flickering red with revenge.

Soldiers

We are a series of circles each pair
In line, dusty ankles marching side by
Side. Dance for me please, within the disco
Lights and shadow being dropped upon tonight's
Sky; lift my limbs. Blankets bellow in a
Cool wind white fire, the salt burying into
Our lips rip words from your once tender song.
Tiny feet climb beat against each rib in turn
Little hands clamber hungry for confession,
The stones tumble hours drop and unravel
The soil our witness, this farm our right to freedom.

Amid

Melodies pace the night
Weave slowly within the echoes
Servants to the stars children of the moon;
Stand frozen feel the dark tides writhe
Their hollow yet still heavy eyes fall
Land accusingly upon us.

Golden sunlight melts like
Liquid through the clouds, surrounds us
Diligently descends suspended by peace;
Squint carefully and you can see it flinch
Inch away from the pain let tears fall
With reluctance retreat.

Grey pavements stalk our knees our fragile feet
in pieces have already given in to
the endlessness of concrete. Compromised
crowds of shallow shoulders step in-between
the falling rain towards another day.
Drawing to a close the sky grows orange.

Can hear tunnels creeping
Through the twisted branches of trees
Crawling shyly beneath the restless breeze;
Look long enough and you will see roots twitch
From the depths of their unrest set rise
Gentle waves from the soil.

Pebbles whisper within
The ocean calm as a puddle
Roll soulfully to the clapping of limbs;
With patience wait and slowly you'll perceive
The bodies of those grown tired rise
At last be laid to rest.

Carpenters

Yet another loop hole born
from the threads of our sunshine.
Songlines only a whisper
and I.

But the circles while you sing
and their contours rise; lift then disappear
can only skim across the surface.
Our matchsticks do still burn within the sky

and so our blood cells still set each evening
red upon the white bruises; until blackened again,
bodies curled,
yet another knot tied.

Slowly it peels;
our pale skin.

Nothing

a teardrop fallen.
Children play now upon fishing nets,
the salty mesh of a blind man's eye.
Insistence speaks freely
since the death of Mnemosyne
and her daughters pine.
Grown shy the acquaintance
in whose weathered anatomy we once perpetuated time.
Sun-bleached our carcass curls with the waves
afraid of nothing
as the water retracts
reveals a rocky plateau.
Her words the last to drain through stone.

In Silence

In silence listen
to all of the repetition all
of the beating hearts
to their gentle percussion as they
colour the heaving
of times rhythmic bass follow the flow
of events explode
in chorus before fading away
as diligently
they witness the existence of moods
moments and fragile
days. Over and over and again.

Autumn

Wallflower

Heels against an old stone wall
she sits, the whiskey within her weathered hands,
tiny as a shadow born beneath the leaf of a magnolia tree
against the bellow of the land.
The rains drum
and the sun it squints with me
succumbed to the hum of the water's wings; my love
she sings bluntly.

Tonight

Asleep the night settles in all around
as the stars yawn at your subtle rise and fall.
It's silent the world tonight, rich with perfect;
forget the hour, even the flowers still grow
twist themselves around you like liquorice
like mist your silhouette drifts gently.
A solemn melody
beautiful within the darkness.

The Diminished

That moment of confluence past,
only a diligent reflection of the stars
upon our clear skin contrasts these currents of feeling
creeping between us.
A voice drifts in the dark,
cold as the moon quiet as the arch of a fin
callous as the cracks appearing
from within the beds of our lips;
a sun-dried apathy.
Stagnant puddles litter the fall of each balding crest
the dissolution of the lightness of our veil
the birth of legs.
As if a tear, cast beneath the yellow of morning
your silver blanched, a glassy silhouette.
Our blood riven a river silenced returned to the air
an echo of despair and the weight of my steps.

Forever

The way that we drip patiently from each other
Still slide tender with honey coloured fingernails
Down each others cheeks continues to amaze;
Even after all the words we've exchanged

Our eyelashes can't keep from splashing. Cold toes grip
Nakedly to the scattering of beached stones
Grown restless their bellies beat upon the fallen grief;
Is it luck that binds us or honesty

That has left these scars upon my skin? Often lost
And filled with innocence the mornings are not
As gentle as they used to feel anymore
For no longer do we read to each other

Fairytales at bed time. All the blossom has fallen
From our tree and snaked into the breeze below.
Within the silence though our red lips release
Love still hearts still pump each others warm blood.

Autumn Breeze

Soft and patient the sky lends itself to
another pair of apprehensive brown eyes.
The woods collectively sigh; nothing's new.

The leaves whisper amongst themselves cast clues
like rain a spiteful game, at which the sky
though so soft and patient lends itself too.

Tears creep peacefully cradled softly by you,
entwined limbs can't shiver but still our lashes fly,
the woods collectively sigh; nothing's new.

Pure white clouds hold hands within the blue
but tonight's black is the only colour without lies.
Soft and patient the old sky lends itself to

today's deceit. This peace beautiful but untrue.
Iris to iris we wait our pupils wide with why,
the woods collectively sigh; nothing's new.

It doesn't matter how tight I hold you
this autumn's breeze has already begun its goodbye,
soft and patient as our sky lends itself to
the old woods collective sigh; nothing's new.

Forget

The clouds have finally swallowed me.
After so many years patience
I'm sorry,
but my promises are still falling
rhythmic and steady.
Won't you let your weight rest soft and heavy upon the cold sea
and drift gently from shore.
As delicate as this morning's call
of mist and angel gathering you'll wake warm from trembling
remember nothing of before.

The End

There'll be no sleep tonight.
It's much too quiet an autumn this year
for forgiveness, the air already empty
of leaves the shadows now only ash in wind.

Instead, you cast your eyes
down your shy face and dirty blonde dripping.
Dead within your hands two salty pools
of foolishness, two foetus of understanding.

This is how much it costs
a true tattoo upon skin.
From the silence your frame hangs
question marked by the beautiful shapes of your limbs.

There'll be no sleep tonight.
It's much too quiet an autumn this year
for forgiveness,
for love.

Deserted

Spilling onto the streets
my missing you creeps out from inside
before treating the day to a piece of my mind.
Beauty rips down flowering backdrops and melody scolds the sky
while peaceful thoughts vanquish the anguish behind salt filled eyes.
I love you
echoes silently
from every discarded clock's jolting hand,
raindrops paint the land
it's deserted now
this town.

Oxford

Her blonde pours from the great doors
and from the windows, falls
from the lamps hung like my head
at this hour,
carves a path straight through the absence of light.
Not a single car nor even a voice,
only my shadows sow time tonight.

The air rakes at my feet as I drag them
through the invisible scores of braced eyes
all been planted deep within our history.
A mutany of mind.

It's soft the sunlight but cold and so old
and it sings while this morning attempts to rise
lullabies above the slow forming crowds.
Inside my distance I sit. Wait once again
watch hidden by tired. Have been given
another day on which to pray that I'll find you.

My Nights Now

Stolen my sanity with your seductive eyes
The pleasure of craving your touch
Holding you moulding our thighs
Soulful sighs heavy with warmth
Slow and hungry haunt my nights
Now I'm without you

Honest

A slow ember. The night squirms
and turns mercilessly,
a congruent of truth.

Five soldiers,
white flag above their heads:
my ethereal trail,
a tail to their inky footsteps.

Bold and mellow the landscape
debris beneath the thorns.
Within autumns orchard, an uprising,
hang mutiny's silenced wings.

Rebel. Hold me
aloft; a peace offering my sunrise,
my sunset.

I Don't Suppose Yellow Raindrops

I don't suppose yellow raindrops
Will ever displace the blue?

Winter

Passenger

The black thud of the railway track
Tramples up and down my spine
Has hollowed out my eyes. Watching
The temporary forests fill with time
Before leaving me on my own again.
Roots set deep inside the concrete.

How hard would it be
To pull away from me leave
My body swaying staring at the tides of skin
And the flashes of teeth,
The shapes elbows make
Rusty some still clean. Just maybe

Someday the rhythm will ease
Lead me from the dry scraping of my brush
The slapping of pigeon feet: towards home
tears fill the gaps in-between
each black thud of my fingertips upon the keys.
It's my melody they share
Standing there all alone.

Out of Season

Black fingernails twist around her wrists curl
into snail shells,
while eyelids heavy and hung low smother each smile
as it grows from beneath her lips.

It is too early in the day for teeth
and for tongue,
for words: another morning has begun
its cold scolded my ears again,
stolen my love.

Slices of silence
strung from hooks
been pushed out into the porch,
decorate her doorstep so often these days.

Song

A breeze blows
from the broken rhythm of her eyelashes.
Water cupped within her hands.
The birds sing upon their branches
as today dips below the surface

forefinger poised.
The walls envelopes
soft as liquid he slips out from inside
while the record continues to spin.
All sound drowned by the backdraft of our blades.

Melody begins again as the postman walks away.
His needle held firm by our mechanical arms
still supplying demand. Rubble and carpet
and circles spread out across the surface.
A full moon

finally settles within the sky
her reflection returned to the lake.
Lungs hum and the werewolves run away.
A child's face from upon out stretched palms
laid cradled within the grass.

Anniversary

So easy it becomes
to pass over moments,
my hands don't know where to begin.

Cluttered tables ache from celebration
while dripping taps and steaming clothes decorate the quiet
of our home, growing hungry,
growing dark and hollow, slim and perfect.

My pointed ribs, as always
accusing. Was it this
that I've been working for?
Below the watching clouds,
this nicotine bliss filled night?

Why shouldn't we mark such an occasion?
Behind the slow rumble of traffc,
beneath the beautiful throb of yellow lamp shade
our whispers still crawl,
still hum despite the weight.

Evening's sigh? Or am I
once again just passing,
my eyes as ever dead silent?

Mushroom

Wells of promise the wombs of your eyes,
those glassy, noir eyes,
gifts of a muse.

Vines creep from your fingertips,
their smoky halos barbed wire against the soft underbelly of my wrists.
Such substance
within your angled limbs as if a statuette
beneath willowed wings.

Lips to a cigarette, palm to throat,
tongue, witch, mushroom,
the orbit of desire more beautiful than hope.

This Year

This year's age
sits triumphantly upon our chests.
Our eyes broken
minds finally in check.
Juxtaposed with the sky 'I'
begins to grovel.

We are though
like the clouds, all as beautiful,
all bound to the same fate.
Not only by the burden of rebellion but also
by the climate of today's tolerance,
by the plastic of the gloves that offer aid.

Flat on our backs
lifting dandelions towards the moon,
their stems held gently between the rubber of our shoes
we bathe beneath the entrails of our youth;
where once upon a time damp hair licked our noses
and the sun scorched our skin;
where once upon a time
our juxtaposition was with a much greater thing.

Our

The dark has lifted
but the fields remain quiet,
snow so unexpected. Pure.
The sun has only just begun in the sky,
our kitchen light cold still
as the mourning air.

At least sleep treats us all a little more fairly
I suppose, this side of the window
the wallpaper and cutlery and the television
the curtains have begun to glow.
Head in my lap and it's raining now
down upon her eyelashes
all crowded around,
protectors of the peace.

A line of shallow footprints
and the lick of my shadow,
the only sounds out here while she waits;
      with warmth and silence and
            our memories to satisfy this old morning
              so carefully fallen;
for the milk bottles to call.

Tomorrow

The day has broken
its black yolk finally spilt over the contours of your lips,
of your tears
grown too heavy even for the close of your eyes.
Leaves from the moon's milky skin have begun
tumbling in the sky.
Why tonight had to fall at all . . .
call so early the stars from the sun?
Long and lamenting
steam climbs from my coffee cup.

Puddles for Madeleine

It smells like burning.
A child's handwriting
discolours the wall.
Blades turn and circle upon the lawn.
Leaves drop
dead to the floor.
Teeth smash together, tongue
spilling melody
street lamps hum;
pollinate the pavement.
Puddles for Madeleine

gathering upon the surface
oil beds dark as stars.

Hostage

Stolen by the soles of your shoes
Lifted without witness
I belong to you

Standing there
A settlement beyond the skyline.
A chimney's smoke.
Through the window
My eyes swallow let go again
Of a little more each time.

Children spill out onto the street
And your strings fold, limbs
Collapse. Snowfall and footprints.

Blood red curtains:
Only walls this winter.
Skin and bone and
Silence within the medina.
Train tracks but I only circle each night
Right through you.

Cot Death

Her muddy,
Dark brown eyes,
Climb reluctantly towards the stars
As the moon begins asking those questions again.
Freckled with subtle clusters of the past
Her delicate face paces the night,
Impatient yet still too frightened to smile
At him and all he could do to console her
With kisses,
Like wishes born too early

In Passing

And so it becomes
easier to question the silence
when the drums have stopped,
casualties fallen quiet.

Above, their wings will beat with my each breath
their feathers lift and fall with my chest
my only regret,
her blood the weight that's now running from me;

let her clouds of soil absorb the thickness
of time, a red coil around her finger.
Limbs of flame boil the dark and slender air
where in sleep the nights have never held
aloft your black veil

and so it becomes:
everything is as nothing is, both impossible.

Spring

Waiting Room

A witness
to the temperance of need,
the slow passing of endurant hands.

Forgiveness speaks,
but always softly and without assurance
though her words often trace the sun.

Understanding the sea
of momentary indifference
becomes an allude to peace,
becomes fraught with patience
and donates grace to our patchwork of sleep.

Let tomorrow whisper of sentiment,
wash clean the reverent masking of our hours.

Once Upon a Time

Words are learning finally
how to fall gracefully to drum the ground gently
and in time.
So perfectly they slip
from beneath our red tongues and white teeth,
that now they swim silently as subtle and simple sounds
within the rhythm of the crowds; which were
once upon a time
so much fun to come up against.

Skin

If change doesn't make me it will no doubt break me
as its new sky settles in all around.
But just as I get the urge for going
and the sun begins to fall,
just as I heave my limbs finally
from upon my favourite spot and the winds gently begin to rock,
I witness this moment
this fragile soon to be forgotten time.
I listen to each second's requiem
from beneath a failing light,
I tear myself carefully from your touch.
For time has at last drained from between our fingers
like falling grains of sand;
been of no less importance
of no less significance
than the passing rains before summers land.

Often Makes Me Wonder

And it
often makes me wonder
why? Before lying at my feet,
those whispers that sip on the rain
that float on the breeze:
as they so carelessly tumble by
why they tickle my ears as they fall from the sky?
Why they need call me at all?
Haunt me even when I'm so tired?

Memories

I have listened to your parting.
To each drip's thud as it returned to the sea.
But still whenever the wind blows my hollows
breathe. A momentary resurrection
in which my blood also waves,
makes to leave.

Always

Whether stumbling over words
or tripping over time,
rolling around silence
or dancing through the night
there you are in the morning;
like the yellow warming my hands
like the beautiful simplicity that paints this land
breaks the raindrops and slows the breeze.
There you are in the morning,
like the scent of the dew
like the wrinkles upon my skin.

All I Want

I want to write about new skies and about how the sun shines
about birds and their song;
about how the world gently rocks
from yellow to blue
and back again.
I want to become a hello
feel as precious as a goodbye,
drift amongst the words of today
though the news is sometimes so sad.

These Days

How many more days will be made like these
like the mellowness of this breeze?
Rolling towards the ocean ourselves on the wind are free
free to laugh and to see
all the mountains and the stones,
the scenery over which lives have blown, lived and grown;
over which so many times we've spoken of home.

The Kaleidoscope Sky

Under the 'Kaleidoscope Sky'
Nobody sighs because the sun never goes down
Instead it just hangs around,
Chatting aimlessly and carelessly about nothing much at all.
Meanwhile, words like
how your eyes seem to be smiling so perfectly this morning
and of the colour yellow flow
from every peaceful face.
Friends never vanish because the light never breaks
and so love lasts forever;
calmness is our pillow
the insecurity of bees now only for show
as they sew flowers into the air,
petals reassuring falling warming everyone everywhere.
All you need do is sleep
no repayment required
here the melodies are free.

Finally Falling Through the Flames

Opening up all around above below me
clear blue beautiful memories are finally being set free,
at last released from the questioning violence
the threatening self pity so cynical.
Free to float peacefully
amongst the slowly dancing leaves of trees amongst
the heavy raindrops that occasionally paint lazily over our sunny days.
Free now
without any perception of possibility
to be,
        just imagine;

how boundaries would walk talk between themselves
gossip and bow their gaze as we passed:
proposing subtlety but beneath our eyelids secretly smiling
wickedly giggling amongst those without the capacity to
ever know the forbidden rhythm of our resilience,
ever feel the warmth that only ashes could sow.

For we are finally falling through the flames
the demands they make.
Their temperamental
yellow fighting flirting
hallucinogenic above real love could only ever aspire to,
look tired compared to,
the strength of our quiet,
our burning,
passionate silence smouldering pure white

the scorching heat of its reassurance
branded deep within us.

Like You

I like thinking of you
It kind of eases the blue.
Makes the world seem an easier place to stay
when I can collect your kisses and gather your smiles
let your eyes take me away;
and just as thoughts of you fill my head
it's like hearing an echo of the most beautiful words ever said
if ever I'm alone a while.
It's almost as if,
like a simple rhyme happily collides
everything's fine when I'm with you.

Midnight

She looks
smiles so beautifully
cinnamon settles upon her tongue.
Angels tickle my fingertips
seep into the night
as we dance
a shy iris in her left eye.
Already begun
to take flight midnight and still
I can see the sun.